REMEMBERING LIGHT

REMEMBERING

LIGHT

POEMS BY

MARY PATRICIA MENGATO

PHOTOS BY

LARRY RIPPEL

COVER DESIGN BY

ROBIN BRUNELLE

RESPONSES TO REMEMBERING LIGHT

"*Remembering Light is delightful, refreshing- elemental. This collection that calls us to remember unity in the face of current divisiveness comes not a minute too soon.*"

— Sara Connell
*Bestselling author and
founder of Thought Leader Academy*

"*Remembering Light is a beautiful interweaving of nature and movement inspiration focusing on oneness. It is a balance of accessible images and stream of conscious abstraction. I feel the author's deep connection with movement that encourages me to pay more attention to mine. The book contains many gems like the "eyes of the heart" and "inviting, uniting, exciting." The poems are authentic and affirming…just let them wash over and nurture you.*"

— Karen Litzinger, MA, LPC
*Author of recently released "Help Wanted:
An A to Z Guide to Cope with the Ups and Downs of the Job Search"*

"*Mary Patricia's poems, "Remembering Light," are sensory gifts to be read aloud, savored and engaged…here is what opened up for me when I did so.*

Awareness #1: "Creation wants us to live the way that these poems demonstrate, inhabiting receptive perceptive bodies, being fully connected and responsive to the high intelligence of Nature."

Awareness #2: "Creation needs us to become as these poems demonstrate, capable of empathically embodying Creation's mysteries, and amplifying them, as Divinely Aware Humans who celebrate and exalt Creation, and provide attentive care to Life."

Awareness #3: "To hear my own voice reading these poems aloud is to open deeper and deeper into Creation, uniting with Creation, to return radiant with remembering that which I had been seeking."

Engage these magnificent poems with your voice and body, and discover what opens for you."

— Victoria Hanchin, MSW,
Author of "The Seer and The Sayer:
Revelations of The New Earth," retired Wholistic Psychotherapist.

"An invitation to reading as a contemplative practice, this collection of poems, infused with the wonder of life, expresses tactile moments of rapport with natural forces. Each poem draws the reader into the experience of expanding and release inspired by the principles of Unity in Motion."

— Lisa Mertz, PhD, LMT,
Former editor Anthropology of Consciousness;
bodywork practitioner.

"Enter into these poems as a dancer in a room that is slowly dissolving into light. Let them draw you into Mengato's numinous mysticism as you join her on the dance floor to experience unity with cosmic geometry, or one danced moment merging with all moments, or the extraordinary light that breaks through when a dancer is both moving and centered at the same time. Don't look for these miracles... Just dance with her. They will come to you."

— Rev. Gail Sofia Ransom DMin

REMEMBERING LIGHT

Copyright © 2022 by Mary Patricia Mengato

To request permissions, contact the publisher at
contact@freedomhousepublishingco.com or rememberinglight22@gmail.com

Hardback ISBN: 978-1-952566-83-7
Paperback ISBN: 978-1-952566-77-6
Printed in the USA.
Freedom House Publishing Co
Middleton, ID 83644
www.freedomhousepublishingco.com

FREEDOM HOUSE
PUBLISHING CO

DEDICATION

This book is dedicated to Sister Mary Louis, who introduced me to the joy of poetry in sixth grade, and whose spirit encouraged me to discover and persevere through writing these poems.

And to Gaia, the earth mother of us all.

TABLE OF CONTENTS

ACKNOWLEDGEMENTS

First of all, I would like to acknowledge with infinite love and gratitude, Larry, my partner in life and love, for bringing the photos in this book into being, and for holding my hand through this whole journey.

Secondly, special thanks to Janet Seltman for ongoing support, and for putting the wild idea of writing a book into my imagining in the first place.

Of course, I give endless appreciation to Cristiam Nebadon for his dedicated and loving teaching of Unity in Motion, and to the Unity in Motion community and other dear friends for encouragement. Special thanks to my daughters Elena and Julia for love, tech support, and helpful feedback, and to Victoria Hanchin for advice and cheerleading.

Heartfelt gratitude to Dawna Markova for those many long ago lessons in trusting my mind and heart.

Many thanks to kind and intrepid writing teachers Jacki Lyden and Eric Weiner for getting me started on the art of developing a writing practice at the Colton House Writing Retreat.

Also, so much appreciation and credit goes to Keira Poulsen of Freedom House Publishing Co. for her online book writing course and encouraging coaching.

And to Sara Connell for inspiration and for her generous online writing webinars.

Finally, I extend many thanks to Robin Brunelle for the beautiful cover design, and to Claire Ormsby and the team at Freedom House Publishing Co. for guiding me through the publishing process.

INTRODUCTION

I have always loved the feeling of space. As a child the expanse of the night sky, the upward reach of trees, and the endless horizon of ocean and beach gave me a freedom and lightness of being that I never felt in my daily life as a city kid. Nature spoke to me of other worlds of wonder and possibility I could hardly imagine. Growing up, this lightness was a rare experience as I focused on school and then a career in dance.

Dancing was how I felt connected to myself and to space.

Fast forward through dance training and career, a change of direction with other movement and body/energy work training, to a lecture given by the founder of Unity in Motion. At the time I was looking for a new movement discipline and when Cristiam Nebadon began the lecture by showing pictures of the earth and its relation to the cosmos, I was hooked. The idea of moving with the whole universe was new and exciting to me, and so I began years of studying and teaching Unity in Motion.

My awareness and experience of myself and of the natural world was profoundly changed by practicing the movements of the

Unity in Motion form and its principles of geometry and consciousness. The foundation of the work is the understanding and experience of moment-to-moment union with all of creation and with the expression of physical life as divine love. Through this practice I began to experience a new way of perceiving myself as simultaneously physical, energy, movement, space, and light.

It continues to be a process of ongoing discovery and creativity.

This book arrived as a vision through the heart-mind of a friend. She saw my photographer husband, Larry, and I working together on a book about Unity in Motion and Nature. The moment Janet told me about the vision, my whole being felt a 'yes'. Larry immediately agreed and we both began the journey that became this book. I had never considered myself a writer, but the 'yes energy' we both felt around the idea was so clear it only remained to discover how this would happen.

The universe provided an unexpected opportunity for travel west to a writing workshop, and so I began my writing practice. My writing gradually morphed from explanation to the rhythm, imagery, and holistic nature of poetry.

My intention in writing these poems was to convey the feelings of expansion, rhythmic flow, connection, and energy of the Unity in Motion movements; encouraging an inner journey into the divine beauty and magic of physical life. My hope is that the reader receives the poems in a way that opens and encourages a uniting of thinking, feeling, and physical embodying, as a union with one's true nature as light.

As with all poetry it is best to read it aloud, to experiment with different phrasing, and to enjoy levels of wordplay and meaning.

The photographs are a visual immersion in Nature as light, the perception of beauty as illumination.

Unity in Motion exists as a field of love and unity expressing as beauty and ongoing creation. I invite you, dear reader, to enter this field and to experience and remember the love and light of your being in oneness with the natural world.

BEGIN

Walking into the darkened room
Looking around
Quiet here
Empty
Echoes of long gone voices
Erased
Only shadows of corners
whispering hush
Be still
Velvet air soothing skin and brain
Stopping to feel, to take this in
No references
Blank
Room for breath
for No thing
for Light
a thin slant framing an opening.

MORNING

Radiance
Walking across the room
Meeting the sun
Awakening the sphere
The circumference of the earth
in this space
Moving my arms into the vastness
This moment of connection
Unraveling my heart.

NEW

Sun pulse
Gift of light
Emergent
Hologram of radiance filling space
Geometry of stars
Encountering the solar heart
Filaments reaching the core
Essence of illumination
The eyes of my heart receive the gift
Sharing it with earth's beat
Join the rhythm of ground
Expanding into cells
Remembering their origin
Direct line returning ancient dance
The ecstasy of life's connection
Raising vision beyond horizon
Unseeable wave
Now carries light encoded
Story of a new beginning.

UNION

Earth, foundation, home.
Becoming physical is an act of love.
Gaia offers
I receive, ascending
I offer
She receives, descending
We remember each other
Hearts merge
Engendering life
Raising the fountain
Quickening the spark
The light of being
Infusing the moment
Emerging into life
Reveals the form.
Divine human body
Touches, feels the ground
Moves in earth's rhythms
In cosmic geometries
Alive in the flow of life.
Real, becoming body
Alight as physical universe
Containing the all
Expressing the one.

CONNECTION

The tree moves through me
Its trunk my center
Its roots my foundation
Its branches my movement.
I stand in the circle of its reach
Unfolding through the sap of its life
My energy is the flowering of the earth
Conduit of beauty.

KNOWING

Ever new
this expanding wave
rides the mind.

Current of presence
washing through
particles sliding.

Melting space
carries the spiral
in and out.

Perfection is now
one whole sphere
forever complete.

FOCUS

Two Eyes
Divergent passengers
Carried through the arc of space
Measuring distances
traveled by my limbs, my spine
Registering the path
Meeting the changes
Neural exchange of light
Defining a world
Joining my heart
to my moving mind
Alight in the widening
Perception
Pinpointed to each whole instant
of time
Giving over to flow
It is creation
Now
seen in my heart.

PHYSICAL LIGHT

Ice of disconnect
Points of light sharp frozen in space
Eggshell delicate and strong
To crack would only make more shards
Hold the pattern in confusion
No, touch gently
And immerse it
Water turns and bends the light
Washes through the open spaces
Finds the flow to reconnect
Line to line becomes a circle
Frames the whole
And moves the center
In to out, in all directions
Now a sphere
Gives form to life.
Zero point, a cosmic moment
Space of stillness becomes real
Form to form to form
The moment joins the points
As every path appears
And I appear, eternal, timeless
Present
In the point of flow

All is equal weightless motion
Life, in fullness
Always here
Turning into what is now
The circle
Lives within me

And expands into the all
Edges gone
One movement only
Simultaneous connection
New earth rising to embrace
Light, moving in the joy of living
Loving every moment here.

HERE

All I am is here now
Ticking through each moment
Molded
Carved to the center of space
Becoming anew
Here and Here and Here
Arcing the path
Awaking again
The Here, the Here, the Here
Are you here?
Empty and full
Be Here, be Here, be Here
Eyes open
Spine moving
Releasing the lower, the middle, the upper
A wave, a wave, a wave
I gather my mind
I'm Here, I'm Here, I'm Here
Heart open
Arms spiral
Encircle the centers
Meeting the moment, It's gone
Arrive to now
To Here, to Here, to Here…

SOFTEN

Softening
Mud
Air
Sap
Gaze
Opening into the veil.
Seeing the unseen geometry
Giving structure to the unformed
Pathways appearing as I touch them.
The map defining my center line
Ascends and descends with me
Embracing me from all directions
A moving template
Shaping me.

DEEPENING

Gravity transforming
No weight here
Passing through here
Each frame a new whole.
Following the rhythm
An even flow to
The center of space
A moving core
expanding within
Suspending all weight
A zero point transfer
Pathway of light
Leading into the center.
Arriving is changing
Not stopping keeps moving
The up is the down
The down is the up
All meet in the center
The core always inner
The edge always outer
The movement the center
Creating, deepening
Lightness of being.

MAGNETIC

Arriving at central heart
Electric moment
Passing fingers to fingers
The touching of halves
Two eyes, two sides
of my heart.
Expanding hemispheres uniting
Whole right
Whole left
All above
All below
Radiant life
in all directions
Inner cosmos
Heart of the sphere
Eternal.

FOUNTAIN

Spring ever present
Full fountain
Raises and circles
Full fountain
God's heart is my heart
Full fountain
Lifts all to the crown
Full fountain
Goes spiraling in
Full fountain
Inner heart opens
Full fountain
Is one with Earth's heart
Full fountain
Descends to arise
Full fountain
Awakens the Self
Full fountain
Receiving the gift
Full fountain
While sharing it back
Full fountain
Return to the source
Full fountain
That never runs dry
Full fountain
The center of life
Full fountain
Forever renewed
Love's fountain.

ANSWER

"Will it be in love?" you ask
Reverberating my whole being awake
Love?
The only reality there is
Hidden in plain sight
Under words that deny it
Yet it lives
In pages still to be written
Heard across eons
Disguised
Waiting to be discovered
Where it always was, is,
"Yes, it will be in love,
It is in love"
Living in the very form
Lit into being
Every step on the path
As I view it
Illuminated in rays going deep to the core
Of life.
The flower repeats and grows the seed
Receives the light, love's form appearing
All is love and love's reflection
Knows the words
And speaks the answer
Pulsing an infinite yes.

BEAUTY

Flowers know
the secret of beauty
is love.

SOFT PALETTE

Soft palette, this
Arched roof curving towards
Lengthening
Circling into vertical
Ground descending
Feet called into earth
Embraced
to the center (of the universe)
This expanding wave
Ever coming, ever going
Formless forming
of life, of being
Renewing the line
Only to move
Only to move
Unwinding the vines
Freeing the blossom
the delicate pathway
of strength
Weaving a smile.

EARTH

Spirit is ripe here
Tasting of moss softened ground
Moist leaves envelope trees
Amplify my awareness.

Distinct harmonic drop
Shifts space to a sphere.
Air rides the wave of my arms
Sun dipped rocks ride the ongoing water
I am in the flow
Immersed in the center of emerging life
Trees bridge the distance
Create the path of grounding this magic
Inviting
Uniting
Exciting
The way is clear
To find the center
The place of ease appears in moments
Two streams becoming one
Sky in water
Earth in me
Sphere of Venus touched in hand

Focus shift

A wider lens sees all directions
Shifts the balance
Turns the sphere
Shows the form of Presence here
Stillness lives inside the tree
The moment
Life
Returns
The circle
Earth unfolds her next creation
Sun embraces earth to moon
Sitting in the moving center
Spirit opens contemplation
Deity, the inner mountain
Crowns the earth
Infolding splendor
Matches
Sources
Dances
And the path keeps moving onward
Follows one line in the pattern
Where all lines make up the whole.

Savor the fruit.

.

PRACTICE

Resistance
is subtle
a barely noticeable pressure
behind my heart.
It pushes forward
A brace against being too soft
An interruption
A disconnect
My spine misses a beat
in the unfolding rhythm of the wave.
I forget to breathe.

Earth comes into my awareness
I lie in the sphere of her gravity,
Descend from my center line
into the space under her surface,
Ascend from my center line
Into the space above her,
My curves are suspended
I am weightless on the ground
Soften into weightlessness
Supported.
Legs extending long and free
Arms moving from my heart
Present mind
Only this flow
Releasing each moment
The next moment coming
No effort needed
The ongoing rhythm
Is one with my heart.

PLACE OF BALANCE

In the center of space lies infinity
Holographic continuum of existence
Space within space
Time within time
Life within life
I stand in the center.

In the center of form lies space
Omnidirectional opening of awareness
Form within form
Pattern within pattern
Expansion within expansion
I move in the center.

In the center of movement lies stillness
Eternal presence of oneness
Movement within movement
Spiral within spiral
Center within center
I Am in the center.

Center of love

Center of beauty

Center of freedom.

FABRIC OF LIFE

Invisible threads crossing space
The lines connecting branch to branch
Carve the air, carve the tree
Ground beneath
Is close, runs deep
Deep to the mountain
That holds this field
This tree holds me
Limb to limb, umbrella seat
I watch the wind
In weightless state
A balance that is free
Free to the air
Spinning the leaves, merry circles
Dancing the tree, defining orbits
Self-contained
Within the limitless universe

A crossing over seems unlikely
I am happy to stay here
Pushing will not move the river
Simply open to its flow
A full embrace, the sphere encircles
Connects above, connects below
Hidden spider knows the weave
And follows all the lines directions
Maps of music, seen, not heard
Vibration shaping worlds in motion

Forms align, wise woman sits
In the presence
Life suspending
Time has shifted to eternal
Every moment threads the needle
I am moving in the eye.

QUANTUM

Space
Full of itself
Me full of it
Limitless bounty in each atom
Fractals repeating in stories
of life
Born in earth's heart
Cosmic seeds imagining form
in vibration
Elemental essence
Pervading each paradigm
I am ignited through my core
A starburst blazing sun
In holographic miniature
Seeing the whole universe
Moving
In waves of light
Light
Full of space
Me full of it
Space
Full of light
Me full of it.

VISTA

Bright relentless sun,
No cloud,
Scouring me clean.

Dry red ground,
Powder dust rock,
Spare green.

Still distance.

Space.

Depth of field.

I enter
the horizon,
Center of my chest expanding
matching this open vision
this rock rooted grounding.
Mind awakening
Channels of energy
Inner form, outer form
moving as one.

The distance enters me
Equal to my entering,
Exposing inner space.

Entrancing mirror,
echo for my eyes
Reflecting vast illusions
Ringing layers peel
Surrounding the mountain.

I sit.
Quiet deity.

UNBOUND

Shedding the skin to look with eternal eyes
Unbound by time or place
To see the new earth forming
Her heart of crystal light
Transforming solid ground beneath
To stand in the center of space
Discovering the unlocking
Word she knew before
The sound of creation
Rang in beauty
To remember existence.

GLORIOUS

Ecstatic shedding of color
Giving the season away
Swept in glory of ground
Gold shine
Returns the warmth
Glowing upward
Florescence plays
Opens delight in eyes
Reminds me
of Joy
Nature knows she is becoming alive
The universe dances in cycles
Loving its own beauty awake
in Heart's mirror,
Rejoices the moment I recognize it.

SIMPLE TRUTH

Love reveals itself
Creating new life
Recognizes itself
In the blooming
Exists as the only
Form
Exquisite rose of the heart
Center of the universe
Love is the ancestor renewing the future now.

DANCE

Delight shines through every fiber
Touched by unexpected magic
Fields of play surround me
Calling me to see how
Each part appears in turn
A new design of color
Appearing to tell of joy opening
the way home
A garden within awakens the bare branches
Into knowing their desire is
to be transformed
As light reveals their inner form
My winter heart
Sees what is real
Dimensions merge, a new earth enters
This walk through my body
Laughing with life
Moving in circles that open
The moment
In presence.

BIOGRAPHIES

Mary Patricia Mengato is passionate about sharing creative, fully embodied, and nature-connected movement experiences with people of all ages and abilities. A Unity in Motion teacher, Movement Artist, and Body/EnergyWork Practitioner, this book is her first foray into sharing through poetry. Mary Patricia loves walking in wide open spaces and planting gardens. She lives in Pittsburgh, PA, with her husband Larry.

Larry Rippel has been active in the arts and photographic community in Pittsburgh for forty years. A freelance photographer since 1994, he specializes in commercial, technological, industrial, editorial, and political photography and has worked for many artists and non-profit arts organizations. His work has been shown locally and internationally.

For inquiries about teaching engagements, classes, and workshops
contact: rememberinglight22@gmail.com

For more information about Unity in Motion see
unityinmotionblog.com

59458908R00045